# SIX FIGURES AND BROKE: BREAKING FREE FROM LIVING PAYCHECK TO PAYCHECK

## I. Introduction

### A. Brief overview of the book's main themes and purpose

The book "Six Figures and Broke" aims to address the common struggle of living paycheck to paycheck despite earning a decent income. It delves into the challenges faced by individuals in this situation and offers practical strategies to break free from the cycle. The main themes of the book include understanding the causes of living paycheck to paycheck, assessing one's financial situation, creating a budget and financial plan, building an emergency fund, tackling debt, increasing income, changing mindset and habits, and building a sustainable financial future. Through a combination of personal stories, research, and actionable advice, this book empowers readers to take control of their finances and achieve long-term financial stability.

### B. Explanation of the significance of living paycheck to paycheck

Living paycheck to paycheck is a significant issue that affects millions of people worldwide. It refers to the situation where individuals or families rely on each paycheck to cover their immediate expenses, leaving little to no room for savings or financial security. The significance of living paycheck to paycheck lies in the following aspects:

1. Financial Vulnerability: Living paycheck to paycheck leaves individuals and families vulnerable to unexpected expenses or emergencies. Without any savings or buffer, a sudden medical bill, car repair, or job loss can cause financial distress and push them deeper into debt.

2. Stress and Anxiety: The constant struggle to make ends meet and the fear of not having enough money for basic necessities can lead to high levels of stress and anxiety. This stress can take a toll on mental and physical health, affecting overall well-being.

3. Limited Opportunities: When most of the income is dedicated to immediate expenses, there is little room for investing in personal growth, education, or career advancement. This can limit opportunities for individuals to improve their financial situation and build a better future.

4. Lack of Financial Freedom: Living paycheck to paycheck means being trapped in a cycle of financial instability. It becomes difficult to save for retirement, invest in assets, or enjoy discretionary spending. This lack of financial freedom can prevent individuals from achieving their long-term goals and dreams.

5. Inter-generational Impact: The impact of living paycheck to paycheck can extend beyond an individual's lifetime. It can perpetuate a cycle of financial instability within families, as children growing up in such circumstances may face similar challenges as adults. Breaking this cycle requires a concerted effort to improve financial literacy and create sustainable financial habits.

Recognizing the significance of living paycheck to paycheck is crucial in order to address the underlying causes and implement strategies to break free from this cycle. It involves building financial resilience, improving money management skills, and creating a solid foundation for long-term financial stability and success.

# II. Chapter 1: The Reality of Living Paycheck to Paycheck

### A. Definition and explanation of what it means to live paycheck to paycheck

Living paycheck to paycheck refers to the situation where an individual or household relies on each paycheck to cover their immediate expenses and has little to no savings or financial cushion. It means that the income earned is entirely or almost entirely spent on essential living expenses such as rent, utilities, groceries, transportation, and debt payments, leaving little or no money left over for savings or discretionary spending.

When someone lives paycheck to paycheck, they often find themselves in a constant cycle of financial constraint. Once they receive their paycheck, they use it to cover their immediate expenses, but as the next payday approaches, they may struggle to make ends meet again. This cycle continues, with each paycheck being fully allocated to cover expenses, leaving no financial buffer for unexpected costs or emergencies.

Living paycheck to paycheck can occur due to various reasons, including low wages, high living expenses, excessive debt, or a lack of budgeting and financial planning. It can affect people from all income levels, including those with low-wage jobs, middle-class families, and even some high-income earners who have high expenses or poor financial habits.

This financial situation can have significant implications and challenges. It leaves individuals and families vulnerable to unexpected expenses or emergencies, causing financial stress and anxiety. It also limits their ability to save for the future, invest in assets, or enjoy discretionary spending. Moreover, living paycheck to paycheck can prevent individuals from achieving long-term financial goals and can perpetuate a cycle of financial instability.

Breaking the cycle of living paycheck to paycheck requires a combination of strategies, including budgeting, reducing expenses, increasing income, and building a savings habit. It involves creating a financial plan, prioritizing expenses, and finding ways to save and invest for the future. By taking steps to improve financial literacy and develop healthy financial habits, individuals can work towards achieving financial stability and freedom.

**B. Statistics and research on the prevalence of this financial situation**

Living paycheck to paycheck is a widespread financial challenge that affects a significant portion of the population. Here are some statistics and research findings on the prevalence of this situation:

1. According to a 2020 survey by the National Endowment for Financial Education (NEFE), nearly 3 in 4 Americans (74%) reported that they were living paycheck to paycheck at least some of the time.

2. The Federal Reserve's Report on the Economic Well-Being of U.S. Households in 2020 revealed that 25% of adults in the United States had no emergency savings at all, leaving them vulnerable to unexpected expenses.

3. A survey conducted by CareerBuilder in 2019 found that 78% of full-time workers in the U.S. were living paycheck to paycheck, an increase from 75% in the previous year.

4. The 2021 Money Mindset Report by Varo Bank revealed that 58% of Americans experienced a financial shock in the last year,

such as a job loss, health emergency, or unexpected expense, which further highlights the lack of financial cushion.

5. A study conducted by the Center for Financial Services Innovation (CFSI) found that 44% of American adults struggled to cover their expenses for at least three months in a row during the year.

6. The 2020 Financial Wellness Survey by PwC reported that 59% of employees in the United States were stressed about their finances, with 49% indicating that their financial stress impacted their work performance.

7. The Economic Policy Institute (EPI) found that the share of working-age families with no retirement savings increased from 31% in 2003 to 41% in 2019, indicating a lack of long-term financial planning and preparation.

These statistics highlight the widespread prevalence of living paycheck to paycheck and the financial challenges faced by individuals and households. It emphasizes the importance of financial education, planning, and building savings to break the cycle of financial instability and achieve long-term financial well-being.

### C. Personal stories or anecdotes illustrating the challenges faced by individuals in this situation

Here are a few personal stories and anecdotes that illustrate the challenges faced by individuals living paycheck to paycheck:

1. Sarah: Sarah is a single mother working two jobs to make ends meet. She struggles to cover basic expenses such as rent, utilities, and groceries. Every month, she finds herself juggling bills and making tough choices about which bills she can afford to pay on time. Sarah often feels stressed and anxious about her financial situation, as she has no savings to fall back on in case of emergencies.

2. John and Lisa: John and Lisa are a young couple who recently graduated from college and entered the workforce. They have student loan debt and are paying off credit card debt from their college years. Despite both of them having full-time jobs, they find it challenging to save money or plan for the future. They often have to forgo vacations or major purchases because their income is primarily allocated towards debt repayment and essential expenses.

3. Michael: Michael is a middle-aged professional who lost his job during the economic recession. He struggled to find employment for several months and relied on unemployment benefits to cover his expenses. As he depleted his savings, Michael fell behind on mortgage payments and accumulated credit card debt. Despite finding a new job eventually, it took him years to recover financially and rebuild his savings.

4. Maria: Maria is a recent college graduate who started her first job in a high-cost city. She quickly realized that her salary was not enough to cover the high rent, student loan payments, and other living expenses. She often finds herself relying on credit cards to make ends meet, which leads to a cycle of debt and financial stress.

These personal stories highlight the financial strain, stress, and difficult choices faced by individuals living paycheck to paycheck. They showcase the need for financial support, budgeting skills, and access to resources that can help individuals break free from this cycle and achieve financial stability.

# III. Chapter 2: Understanding the Causes

### A. Identification and exploration of the common reasons why people find themselves living paycheck to paycheck

There are several common reasons why people find themselves

living paycheck to paycheck. Let's explore some of them:

1. Low Wages: One of the primary factors is low wages. Many individuals work in jobs that pay minimum wage or offer low salaries, making it difficult to cover basic expenses and save money. This is especially true for individuals in entry-level positions or industries that are not well-compensated.

2. High Cost of Living: The cost of living in certain areas, particularly in cities, can be very high. Rent, utilities, transportation, and other essential expenses can consume a significant portion of a person's income, leaving little room for savings.

3. Lack of Financial Education: Many people never received formal financial education and may not have developed the skills to effectively manage their money. This can result in poor budgeting, overspending, and accumulating debt, which can lead to living paycheck to paycheck.

4. Debt and Financial Obligations: Debt can be a major obstacle to financial stability. Student loans, credit card debt, and other financial obligations can consume a significant portion of a person's income, leaving little room for saving or emergencies.

5. Unforeseen Expenses: Unexpected expenses, such as medical bills, car repairs, or home repairs, can quickly deplete a person's savings and force them to live paycheck to paycheck. Without an emergency fund, individuals may struggle to cope with these unexpected financial burdens.

6. Irregular or Inconsistent Income: Some individuals have irregular or inconsistent income, such as freelancers or gig economy workers. This can make it challenging to budget and plan for expenses, leading to a cycle of living paycheck to paycheck.

7. Lack of Access to Affordable Housing: Affordable housing can

be a significant challenge for many individuals and families. High rent prices and a lack of affordable housing options can force people to spend a large portion of their income on housing, leaving little left for other expenses.

These are just a few of the common reasons why people find themselves living paycheck to paycheck. It's important to address these challenges through financial education, improving job opportunities and wages, and creating policies that support affordable housing and economic stability.

### B. Discussion of external factors such as low income, high expenses, and debt

Let's further discuss the external factors that contribute to living paycheck to paycheck:

1. Low Income: Low income is a significant external factor that can limit a person's ability to cover their expenses and save money. It can be due to various reasons such as a lack of job opportunities, limited education or skills, or even systemic factors like the economic conditions of a particular region or country.

2. High Expenses: High expenses, including the cost of housing, utilities, transportation, healthcare, and childcare, can consume a significant portion of a person's income. In some cases, the cost of these essential expenses may exceed the income, leaving individuals with no choice but to live paycheck to paycheck.

3. Debt: Debt, whether it's from student loans, credit cards, medical bills, or other financial obligations, can be a major burden and hinder financial stability. High interest rates and monthly payments can eat into a person's income, making it challenging to break free from the paycheck-to-paycheck cycle.

4. Inflation: Inflation, the increase in the general price level of goods and services over time, can erode the purchasing power of an individual's income. When expenses rise faster than income, it

becomes difficult to maintain a comfortable financial position and save for the future.

5. Unemployment or Underemployment: External factors such as job loss or being underemployed (working part-time or in a job that does not fully utilize skills or qualifications) can greatly affect a person's income and financial stability. It can lead to a reliance on savings or credit, making it harder to break free from living paycheck to paycheck.

6. Healthcare Costs: The rising costs of healthcare, including insurance premiums, deductibles, and out-of-pocket expenses, can put a strain on one's budget. Medical emergencies or chronic health conditions can quickly deplete savings and leave individuals financially vulnerable.

7. Family Responsibilities: Taking care of dependents, such as children or aging parents, can significantly impact a person's finances. The costs associated with raising a family or providing care for loved ones can stretch a budget and make it difficult to save or build financial security.

Addressing these external factors requires a comprehensive approach that includes policies to improve job opportunities, increase wages, provide affordable healthcare and education, and create a supportive social safety net. Additionally, personal financial management skills, such as budgeting, saving, and debt management, can help individuals navigate these external challenges and improve their financial situation.

### C. Examination of internal factors such as mindset, habits, and financial literacy

Let's explore the internal factors that play a role in financial well-being:

1. Mindset: One's mindset and beliefs about money can greatly impact their financial situation. A positive mindset that focuses

on long-term goals, financial independence, and the ability to make sound financial decisions can contribute to better financial outcomes. On the other hand, a negative mindset, such as a fear of money or a belief that financial success is unattainable, can hinder one's ability to improve their financial situation.

2. Habits: Our daily habits and behaviors surrounding money can have a significant impact on our financial well-being. Good financial habits, such as budgeting, saving, and living within one's means, can lead to better financial stability. On the other hand, poor habits, such as overspending, impulse buying, or relying on credit for everyday expenses, can contribute to a cycle of financial stress and living paycheck to paycheck.

3. Financial Literacy: Financial literacy refers to the knowledge and understanding of financial concepts, such as budgeting, investing, debt management, and retirement planning. A lack of financial literacy can make it difficult for individuals to make informed decisions about their money. It is important to develop financial literacy skills through education, self-study, or seeking guidance from financial professionals.

4. Goal Setting: Setting clear financial goals is essential for long-term financial success. Goals help individuals prioritize their spending, save for the future, and make informed financial decisions. Without goals, it can be challenging to stay motivated and make the necessary changes to improve one's financial situation.

5. Self-discipline: Self-discipline plays a crucial role in managing finances effectively. It involves the ability to resist impulsive purchases, stick to a budget, and make wise financial choices. Developing self-discipline can help individuals avoid unnecessary expenses and establish healthy financial habits.

6. Financial Planning: Creating a financial plan is a proactive step towards financial stability. It involves assessing one's current financial situation, setting goals, creating a budget,

and developing strategies for saving, investing, and managing debt. A well-thought-out financial plan can provide a roadmap for achieving financial security and breaking the paycheck-to-paycheck cycle.

7. Continuous Learning: Financial knowledge and the economic landscape are constantly evolving. Engaging in ongoing learning about personal finance, investing, and money management can help individuals adapt to changing circumstances and make informed financial decisions.

By addressing these internal factors, individuals can develop a positive mindset, adopt good financial habits, increase their financial literacy, set clear goals, practice self-discipline, create a financial plan, and continue learning. These actions can significantly improve one's financial well-being and help break free from the cycle of living paycheck to paycheck.

# IV. Chapter 3: Assessing Your Financial Situation

**A. Guidance on how to evaluate and analyze one's current financial state**

To evaluate and analyze your current financial state, follow these steps:

1. Gather Financial Information: Collect all your financial documents, including bank statements, credit card statements, loan statements, investment statements, pay stubs, and any other relevant financial documents.

2. Calculate Net Worth: Calculate your net worth by subtracting your liabilities (debts) from your assets. Your assets may include cash, savings, investments, property, and valuables, while liabilities may include loans, credit card debt, and mortgages. The resulting figure will give you an overview of your overall financial

position.

3. Track Income and Expenses: Review your income sources and track your expenses over a specific period, such as a month. Categorize your expenses into fixed (e.g., rent, utilities) and variable (e.g., groceries, entertainment). This will help you understand where your money is going and identify areas where you can potentially reduce expenses.

4. Assess Debt: Evaluate your debt situation by listing all your outstanding debts, including credit cards, loans, and mortgages. Note down the interest rates and minimum monthly payments for each debt. Assess whether your debt levels are manageable and if any adjustments need to be made to pay off debts more efficiently.

5. Review Budget: Create or review your budget to ensure that your income covers your expenses and savings goals. Compare your actual expenses with your projected budget to identify any areas where you may be overspending or not allocating enough funds.

6. Evaluate Savings and Emergency Fund: Assess your savings and emergency fund to determine if you have enough set aside for unexpected expenses or financial emergencies. Aim to have at least three to six months' worth of living expenses saved in an easily accessible account.

7. Analyze Investments: Review your investment portfolio, including stocks, bonds, mutual funds, or retirement accounts. Assess the performance of your investments and consider if any adjustments are needed to align with your financial goals and risk tolerance.

8. Review Insurance Coverage: Evaluate your insurance coverage, including health, life, home, and auto insurance. Ensure that you have adequate coverage to protect yourself and your assets in case of unexpected events.

9. Evaluate Financial Goals: Review your financial goals and assess your progress towards achieving them. Are you on track, or do adjustments need to be made? Consider short-term goals (e.g., paying off debt) and long-term goals (e.g., retirement savings).

10. Seek Professional Advice: If you feel overwhelmed or unsure about your financial state, consider seeking guidance from a financial advisor or planner. They can provide personalized advice and help you create a comprehensive financial plan.

Remember, financial evaluation and analysis should be an ongoing process. Regularly review and update your financial information to stay informed and make necessary adjustments to improve your financial situation.

### B. Tools and techniques for tracking income, expenses, and debts

Tracking income, expenses, and debts is crucial for maintaining a clear understanding of your financial situation. Here are some tools and techniques you can use:

1. Budgeting Apps: There are various budgeting apps available that can help you track your income, expenses, and debts. These apps often sync with your bank accounts and credit cards to automatically categorize transactions and provide detailed reports. Examples include Mint, YNAB (You Need a Budget), and PocketGuard.

2. Spreadsheets: Using spreadsheet software like Microsoft Excel or Google Sheets allows you to create customized templates to track your income, expenses, and debts. You can set up different sheets for different categories, such as income sources, fixed expenses, variable expenses, and debts. Regularly update the spreadsheet with your financial information to keep it up to date.

3. Envelope System: The envelope system involves allocating cash into different envelopes for specific expense categories. Each

envelope represents a budgeted amount for a particular expense, such as groceries or entertainment. By physically separating your cash into envelopes, you can visually track your spending and ensure you stay within your budget.

4. Expense Tracking Apps: Use expense tracking apps to record your daily expenses. These apps allow you to input transactions manually or scan receipts, categorize expenses, and generate reports. Examples include Expensify, Receipt Bank, and Zoho Expense.

5. Online Banking and Financial Management Tools: Many banks offer online banking platforms that provide detailed transaction histories and spending analysis. These tools can help you track income, expenses, and debts by allowing you to view and categorize your transactions. Additionally, financial management tools like Quicken and Personal Capital can aggregate data from multiple financial accounts for a comprehensive overview.

6. Debt Tracking Spreadsheets: To track your debts, you can create a separate spreadsheet or use debt tracking templates available online. Include details such as the creditor, outstanding balance, interest rate, minimum payment, and due date. Update the spreadsheet regularly to monitor your progress in paying off debts.

7. Manual Tracking: If you prefer a low-tech approach, you can track your income, expenses, and debts manually using a notebook or journal. Write down your income sources, record expenses as they occur, and keep track of your debts by noting balances and payments made.

Whichever method you choose, consistency and regular updates are essential to ensure accurate tracking of your financial information. Find a system that works best for you and make it a habit to review and update your income, expenses, and debts regularly.

### C. Reflective exercises to identify areas for improvement and potential solutions

Engaging in reflective exercises can help you identify areas for improvement and potential solutions. Here are some exercises you can try:

1. Journaling: Set aside dedicated time to reflect on different aspects of your life, such as your career, relationships, health, or personal development. Write down your thoughts, feelings, and observations about each area. Consider what is going well and what could be improved. Explore potential solutions or actions you can take to address any identified areas for improvement.

2. SWOT Analysis: Conduct a SWOT (Strengths, Weaknesses, Opportunities, Threats) analysis for yourself or a specific situation. Identify your strengths and weaknesses, as well as external opportunities and threats. Reflect on how your strengths can be leveraged, weaknesses can be addressed, opportunities can be seized, and threats can be mitigated.

3. Feedback Collection: Seek feedback from trusted individuals such as mentors, colleagues, or friends. Ask them for their honest assessment of your strengths and areas for improvement. Reflect on their feedback and consider how you can incorporate their insights into your personal growth and development.

4. Visualization and Future Self: Visualize your ideal future self in different areas of your life, such as your career, relationships, or personal well-being. Reflect on the gaps between your current self and your future self. Consider what actions or changes you need to make to bridge those gaps and move closer to your desired state.

5. Mind Mapping: Create a mind map to visually explore different aspects of your life or a specific situation. Start with a central concept or goal and branch out to identify different factors, challenges, and potential solutions related to that concept. This

exercise can help you uncover connections and insights that may not be immediately apparent.

6. Prioritization and Time Management: Reflect on how you currently allocate your time and energy. Identify areas where you may be spending too much or too little time, and consider the impact on your overall well-being and effectiveness. Reflect on strategies to better prioritize your time and align your activities with your goals and values.

7. Learning from Mistakes: Reflect on past experiences or mistakes and consider what you have learned from them. Identify patterns or recurring themes that may indicate areas for improvement. Consider how you can apply the lessons learned to avoid similar mistakes in the future.

Remember, the purpose of these reflective exercises is to gain self-awareness and generate ideas for improvement. Be open to exploring new perspectives, challenging assumptions, and considering alternative solutions. Regularly engage in these exercises to continually assess your progress and adapt your approach as needed.

# V. Chapter 4: Creating a Budget and Financial Plan

### A. Step-by-step instructions for creating a realistic budget based on income and expenses

Creating a realistic budget based on your income and expenses can help you manage your finances effectively. Here are step-by-step instructions to guide you through the process:

1. Gather Your Financial Information: Collect all relevant financial information, including your income sources, such as salary, freelance work, or rental income, and your expenses, such as rent/ mortgage, utilities, groceries, transportation, debt payments, and

discretionary spending. Make sure you have accurate and up-to-date information.

2. Calculate Your Total Income: Add up all your income sources to determine your total monthly income. This will give you a clear understanding of how much money you have available to allocate towards your expenses and savings.

3. List Your Fixed Expenses: Identify and list all your fixed expenses, which are regular and consistent payments that don't change much from month to month. This may include rent/mortgage, insurance premiums, loan payments, subscriptions, and other fixed bills. Write down the amount for each expense.

4. Identify Your Variable Expenses: Next, identify and list your variable expenses, which are costs that fluctuate from month to month. These may include groceries, transportation, dining out, entertainment, and personal care. Estimate the average amount you spend on each category based on your past spending habits.

5. Calculate Your Total Expenses: Add up your fixed and variable expenses to determine your total monthly expenses. This will give you a clear picture of how much money you typically spend each month.

6. Determine Your Savings Goals: Consider your financial goals, such as saving for emergencies, retirement, or a specific purchase. Decide how much you want to save each month and prioritize this as an expense in your budget.

7. Evaluate Your Budget: Compare your total income with your total expenses. If your income exceeds your expenses, you have a surplus, which can be allocated towards savings or debt repayment. If your expenses exceed your income, you'll need to make adjustments to your budget by reducing certain expenses or finding ways to increase your income.

8. Make Adjustments: Review your expenses and identify areas

where you can cut back or find more cost-effective alternatives. Look for opportunities to reduce discretionary spending or negotiate lower bills. Consider whether certain expenses are essential or if there are more affordable options available.

9. Allocate Your Income: Allocate your income towards your expenses and savings goals. Start with your fixed expenses, as these are usually non-negotiable. Then, allocate funds towards your variable expenses, ensuring that you stay within your budgeted amounts for each category. Finally, allocate money towards your savings goals.

10. Track and Review: Keep track of your expenses and review your budget regularly. Use a budgeting app, spreadsheet, or a pen and paper to record your expenses and compare them against your budget. This will help you stay accountable and make adjustments as necessary.

Remember, creating a realistic budget is an ongoing process. It may take a few months of tracking and adjusting to find a balance that works for you. Be flexible and willing to make changes as your financial situation and priorities evolve.

## B. Strategies for reducing unnecessary expenses and increasing savings

Reducing unnecessary expenses and increasing savings can help you reach your financial goals faster. Here are some strategies to consider:

1. Track Your Expenses: Start by tracking your expenses to get a clear understanding of where your money is going. Use a budgeting app or simply write down all your expenses for a month. This will help you identify areas where you can cut back.

2. Identify Wants vs. Needs: Differentiate between wants and needs. Focus on covering your essential needs first, such as housing, food, utilities, and transportation. Then, evaluate your

discretionary spending and identify areas where you can reduce or eliminate non-essential expenses.

3. Create a Budget: Establish a budget that aligns with your financial goals. Allocate specific amounts for each category of expenses, including fixed bills and variable expenses. Stick to your budget and regularly review and adjust it as necessary.

4. Cut Back on Eating Out: Dining out and ordering takeout can quickly add up. Consider cooking at home more often and bringing your lunch to work. Pack snacks and drinks when going out to avoid unnecessary expenses.

5. Reduce Subscriptions: Evaluate your subscriptions and memberships. Cancel or downgrade those that you don't use frequently or aren't essential. Consider sharing subscriptions with family or friends to split the cost.

6. Lower Utility Bills: Find ways to reduce your utility bills. Turn off lights and appliances when not in use, adjust the thermostat to conserve energy, and consider installing energy-efficient light bulbs. Also, shop around for the best rates for internet, cable, and phone services.

7. Shop Smart: Comparison shop for groceries and household items. Look for sales, use coupons, and buy in bulk when it makes sense. Consider generic or store-brand products instead of name brands. Avoid impulse purchases and stick to your shopping list.

8. Minimize Impulse Buying: Before making a purchase, take a moment to consider if it's a want or a need. Delay non-essential purchases to avoid impulse buying. Give yourself a cooling-off period to determine if the purchase is truly necessary and fits within your budget.

9. Negotiate Bills and Expenses: Don't be afraid to negotiate bills and expenses. Contact your service providers and ask if they can offer a lower rate or discounts. You may be surprised at the savings

you can achieve just by asking.

10. Increase Your Income: Explore ways to increase your income. Consider taking on a side gig or freelancing, renting out a spare room, or selling unwanted items. Use the extra income to boost your savings or pay off debt faster.

11. Automate Savings: Set up automatic transfers from your checking account to a separate savings account. This way, a portion of your income will be saved before you have a chance to spend it. Treat savings as an expense and prioritize it in your budget.

12. Avoid Impulse Online Shopping: Online shopping can lead to impulse buying. Before making an online purchase, add the item to your cart and wait a day or two. This will give you time to consider if it's a necessary purchase or simply an impulse.

Remember, reducing expenses and increasing savings requires discipline and consistency. Start small, focus on one area at a time, and gradually implement these strategies. Celebrate your progress along the way and stay motivated to achieve your financial goals.

### C. Tips for setting financial goals and creating a long-term plan for financial stability

Setting financial goals and creating a long-term plan for financial stability is crucial for your financial well-being. Here are some tips to help you get started:

1. Define Your Financial Goals: Start by identifying your financial goals. These can include saving for retirement, buying a home, paying off debt, starting a business, or funding your children's education. Be specific about what you want to achieve and set a timeline for each goal.

2. Make SMART Goals: Use the SMART framework when setting your goals. SMART stands for Specific, Measurable, Achievable, Relevant, and Time-bound. This helps you create clear and

actionable goals that will keep you motivated and accountable.

3. Prioritize Your Goals: Determine which goals are most important to you and prioritize them accordingly. You may need to focus on one goal at a time or allocate your resources to multiple goals simultaneously. Consider the urgency, impact, and feasibility of each goal.

4. Assess Your Current Financial Situation: Take stock of your current financial situation. Calculate your net worth by subtracting your liabilities from your assets. Review your income, expenses, and debts. This will give you a clear picture of where you stand and help you make informed decisions.

5. Create a Budget: Establish a budget that aligns with your financial goals. Track your income and expenses to ensure you are spending within your means. Allocate specific amounts for different categories and regularly review and adjust your budget as needed.

6. Build an Emergency Fund: Set aside funds for unexpected expenses in an emergency fund. Aim to save at least three to six months' worth of living expenses. This will provide a safety net and protect you from financial setbacks.

7. Pay Off High-Interest Debt: Prioritize paying off high-interest debt, such as credit cards and personal loans. Make extra payments whenever possible or consider debt consolidation to reduce interest costs. Once you pay off one debt, redirect that payment towards the next one.

8. Save and Invest: Develop a habit of saving regularly. Start with a small amount and gradually increase it over time. Consider opening separate savings accounts for different goals. Additionally, explore investment options that align with your risk tolerance and long-term goals.

9. Review and Adjust Regularly: Review your financial plan

regularly to track your progress and make necessary adjustments. Life circumstances and priorities may change, so be flexible and adapt your plan accordingly. Regularly evaluate your investment portfolio and make necessary changes based on your goals and market conditions.

10. Seek Professional Advice: Consider consulting with a financial advisor or planner to get expert guidance. They can help you create a comprehensive financial plan, provide investment advice, and assist in optimizing your financial strategy.

11. Stay Educated: Continuously educate yourself about personal finance and investment strategies. Read books, attend workshops, listen to podcasts, and follow reputable financial websites. The more knowledge you have, the better equipped you'll be to make informed financial decisions.

12. Stay Disciplined and Patient: Creating long-term financial stability requires discipline and patience. Stick to your plan, avoid impulsive decisions, and stay focused on your goals. Remember that financial stability is a journey, and it takes time to achieve lasting results.

By following these tips and staying committed to your financial plan, you can set yourself up for long-term financial stability and achieve your financial goals.

# VI. Chapter 5: Building an Emergency Fund

### A. Importance of having an emergency fund and its role in breaking the paycheck-to-paycheck cycle

Having an emergency fund plays a crucial role in breaking the paycheck-to-paycheck cycle and ensuring financial stability. Here's why it is important:

1. Financial Safety Net: An emergency fund acts as a safety net to protect you from unexpected expenses or financial emergencies. It provides you with a cushion to cover unforeseen events such as medical emergencies, car repairs, home repairs, or job loss. Without an emergency fund, you may be forced to rely on credit cards or loans, which can lead to debt accumulation and financial stress.

2. Avoiding Debt: An emergency fund helps you avoid going into debt when faced with unexpected expenses. Instead of relying on credit cards or loans, you can use your emergency fund to cover the costs. This prevents the need to borrow money and incur high-interest charges. By avoiding debt, you can maintain financial stability and reduce the financial burden on your paycheck.

3. Breaking the Paycheck-to-Paycheck Cycle: Living paycheck-to-paycheck means relying solely on each paycheck to cover your expenses. This leaves little room for savings or unexpected expenses. By building an emergency fund, you break this cycle by setting aside money specifically for emergencies. It creates a buffer that allows you to handle unexpected expenses without disrupting your regular budget.

4. Peace of Mind: Having an emergency fund provides a sense of security and peace of mind. Knowing that you have funds set aside for emergencies reduces financial stress and anxiety. It allows you to face unexpected situations with confidence, knowing that you have the means to handle them without jeopardizing your financial stability.

5. Independence and Flexibility: An emergency fund gives you financial independence and flexibility. It allows you to make decisions based on what is best for your long-term financial well-being rather than being forced into reactive choices due to a lack of funds. It empowers you to take calculated risks, pursue opportunities, and make necessary changes without being solely dependent on each paycheck.

6. Faster Recovery: When faced with a financial setback or emergency, having an emergency fund enables you to recover faster. Instead of scrambling to find funds or taking on additional debt, you can use your emergency fund to cover the expenses. This allows you to focus on resolving the situation and getting back on track without the added burden of financial strain.

7. Building Financial Discipline: Building an emergency fund requires discipline and consistent saving habits. By prioritizing savings and regularly contributing to your emergency fund, you develop financial discipline and healthy financial habits. This discipline extends to other areas of your financial life, helping you make better decisions and achieve overall financial stability.

In conclusion, an emergency fund is essential for breaking the paycheck-to-paycheck cycle and ensuring financial stability. It provides a safety net, helps you avoid debt, gives you peace of mind, and allows for independence and flexibility. By building an emergency fund, you can handle unexpected expenses and financial emergencies with confidence, ultimately breaking the cycle of living paycheck-to-paycheck.

## B. Strategies for saving money, even on a tight budget

Saving money, even on a tight budget, requires careful planning and discipline. Here are some strategies to help you save:

1. Create a Budget: Start by creating a budget that outlines your income and expenses. This will give you a clear picture of where your money is going and help you identify areas where you can cut back. Allocate a portion of your income towards savings and treat it as a non-negotiable expense.

2. Track Your Expenses: Keep track of your daily expenses to see where your money is being spent. Use mobile apps or a simple spreadsheet to record your expenses. This will help you identify any unnecessary or impulsive spending habits that you can cut

back on.

3. Cut Back on Discretionary Spending: Analyze your expenses and identify areas where you can cut back. This could include eating out less frequently, reducing entertainment expenses, or finding cheaper alternatives for certain products or services. Look for free or low-cost activities and prioritize your needs over wants.

4. Save on Utilities: Reduce your utility bills by being mindful of your energy and water usage. Turn off lights and appliances when not in use, unplug electronics, and consider using energy-efficient light bulbs. Take shorter showers and fix any leaks to reduce water consumption. These small changes can add up to significant savings over time.

5. Meal Planning and Cooking at Home: Eating out can be expensive. Plan your meals in advance, make a grocery list, and cook at home as much as possible. This allows you to control your food expenses and save money. Look for affordable recipes and consider batch cooking or meal prepping to save time and money.

6. Shop Smart: When shopping for groceries or other necessities, compare prices, use coupons, and take advantage of sales and discounts. Consider buying generic or store brands instead of branded products. Avoid impulse buying and stick to your shopping list to avoid unnecessary expenses.

7. Automate Savings: Set up automatic transfers from your paycheck to a separate savings account. This ensures that a portion of your income goes directly into savings before you have a chance to spend it. Start with a small amount and gradually increase your savings rate as your budget allows.

8. Find Ways to Increase Income: Explore opportunities to increase your income, even if it's on a part-time or freelance basis. This could include taking on a side gig, selling unused items, or offering your skills or services. The extra income can go directly towards your savings.

9. Negotiate Bills: Contact your service providers and negotiate better rates for your bills. This could include your internet, cable, or insurance providers. Loyalty doesn't always pay, so don't hesitate to shop around and switch to a provider offering a better deal.

10. Prioritize Saving: Make saving a priority in your financial goals. Treat it as an essential expense and commit to saving a certain percentage of your income each month. Cut back on non-essential expenses and redirect that money towards your savings.

Saving money on a tight budget requires discipline, planning, and a willingness to make changes. By implementing these strategies, you can start building your savings and work towards financial stability, even with limited resources.

### C. Advice on managing unexpected expenses and building resilience

Managing unexpected expenses and building resilience is crucial for financial stability and peace of mind. Here are some pieces of advice to help you in this regard:

1. Build an Emergency Fund: Start by establishing an emergency fund. Aim to save at least three to six months' worth of living expenses. This fund will act as a safety net in case of unexpected expenses such as medical bills, car repairs, or job loss. Save a little each month until you reach your target amount.

2. Prioritize Saving: Make saving a priority in your budget. Allocate a portion of your income towards savings every month, even if it's a small amount. Consistent saving over time will help you build resilience and be better prepared for unexpected expenses.

3. Review Insurance Coverage: Ensure that you have appropriate insurance coverage to protect yourself from major financial setbacks. This may include health insurance, car insurance, home

or renter's insurance, and disability insurance. Review your policies regularly to ensure they adequately cover your needs.

4. Practice Frugal Living: Embrace a frugal lifestyle by practicing mindful spending and living below your means. Cut back on non-essential expenses and find ways to save on everyday items such as groceries, utilities, and entertainment. Reallocate the saved money towards your emergency fund or other financial goals.

5. Create a Contingency Plan: Anticipate potential financial disruptions and create a contingency plan. Identify areas where you can reduce expenses if needed, such as cutting back on discretionary spending or finding alternative sources of income. Having a plan in place will help you respond effectively to unexpected situations.

6. Seek Additional Sources of Income: Consider diversifying your income streams to increase your resilience. Explore opportunities for part-time work, freelancing, or starting a side business. Having multiple sources of income can help mitigate the impact of unexpected expenses.

7. Stay Informed and Seek Professional Advice: Stay informed about financial matters and seek professional advice when needed. Educate yourself on personal finance topics and stay updated on changes in regulations or policies that may affect your financial situation. Consult with financial advisors or experts to get personalized guidance.

8. Maintain Good Credit: Maintain a good credit score by paying your bills on time, managing your debt responsibly, and regularly reviewing your credit report. A good credit score can help you access credit or loans during difficult times and potentially secure better terms.

9. Practice Self-Care: Building resilience goes beyond financial aspects. Take care of your physical and mental well-being to better navigate unexpected challenges. Prioritize self-care activities,

maintain a support network, and seek help when needed. Taking care of yourself will give you the strength to face and overcome financial obstacles.

10. Stay Positive and Flexible: Unexpected expenses are a part of life, and it's important to approach them with a positive mindset and flexibility. Embrace the opportunity to learn from these experiences, adapt your financial strategies if needed, and remain optimistic about your ability to overcome challenges.

By following these tips, you can better manage unexpected expenses and build resilience in your financial life. Remember, it's a journey, and every step you take towards financial stability will contribute to your overall well-being.

# VII. Chapter 6: Tackling Debt

### A. Discussion of different types of debt and their impact on financial well-being

Debt can have a significant impact on an individual's financial well-being. Understanding the different types of debt and their implications can help in making informed financial decisions. Here are some common types of debt and their potential impact:

1. Credit Card Debt: Credit card debt occurs when you carry a balance on your credit card from month to month. Credit cards often have high-interest rates, and if not managed carefully, can quickly accumulate and become difficult to pay off. Carrying a high balance or making only minimum payments can lead to long-term debt and financial stress.

2. Student Loan Debt: Student loan debt is incurred when individuals borrow money to finance their education. Student loans can take years to repay and can affect your ability to save, invest, or achieve other financial goals. It's important to consider the potential impact of student loan payments on your overall financial picture and develop a repayment plan that fits your

budget.

3. Mortgage Debt: Mortgage debt is the amount owed on a home loan. While mortgage debt is generally considered "good debt" as it allows for homeownership and potential appreciation of the property, it still requires careful management. Falling behind on mortgage payments can lead to foreclosure and significant financial consequences.

4. Auto Loan Debt: Auto loan debt is incurred when individuals finance the purchase of a vehicle. While having reliable transportation is essential, taking on excessive auto loan debt can strain your finances. High-interest rates and long loan terms can result in paying more than the vehicle's value over time.

5. Personal Loan Debt: Personal loans are unsecured loans that can be used for various purposes, such as consolidating debt, home improvements, or unexpected expenses. Personal loans typically have fixed interest rates and fixed repayment terms. It's important to borrow responsibly and consider the impact of the loan on your monthly budget and overall financial health.

6. Payday Loans: Payday loans are short-term loans that offer quick access to cash but often come with extremely high-interest rates and fees. These loans can trap individuals in a cycle of debt, as the repayment terms are typically very short, leading to a need for additional borrowing.

The impact of debt on financial well-being depends on various factors, including the amount of debt, interest rates, repayment terms, and an individual's overall financial situation. High levels of debt combined with high-interest rates can lead to financial stress, limited savings, and difficulty achieving long-term financial goals.

To manage debt effectively and improve financial well-being, it's important to:

1. Prioritize Debt Repayment: Make a plan to pay off debt systematically. Consider strategies such as the snowball method (paying off the smallest debt first) or the avalanche method (paying off the debt with the highest interest rate first).

2. Budgeting and Expense Tracking: Develop a budget that allows for regular debt payments while covering essential expenses. Track your spending to identify areas where you can reduce expenses and allocate more towards debt repayment.

3. Negotiate Lower Interest Rates: Contact creditors to negotiate lower interest rates on existing debt. Lower interest rates can reduce the overall cost of borrowing and make debt repayment more manageable.

4. Seek Professional Advice: If struggling with debt, consider reaching out to credit counseling agencies or financial advisors who can provide guidance on debt management strategies, budgeting, and financial planning.

5. Build an Emergency Fund: Having an emergency fund can help prevent the need to rely on credit during unexpected financial situations. Aim to save three to six months' worth of living expenses in an easily accessible account.

Remember, managing debt requires discipline, patience, and a long-term perspective. By understanding the impact of different types of debt and implementing strategies to reduce and manage it effectively, you can improve your financial well-being and work towards a more secure financial future.

## B. Techniques for managing and reducing debt, including debt consolidation and negotiation

Managing and reducing debt requires careful planning and disciplined financial habits. Here are some techniques that can help:

1. Create a Budget: Start by creating a comprehensive budget that includes all your income and expenses. This will give you a clear picture of your financial situation and help you identify areas where you can cut back on expenses to allocate more money towards debt repayment.

2. Prioritize Debt Repayment: List all your debts and prioritize them based on factors like interest rates, outstanding balances, and minimum payments. Consider using the debt snowball method, where you focus on paying off the smallest debt first, while making minimum payments on other debts. Once the smallest debt is paid off, roll that payment into the next debt, and so on. This method provides a sense of accomplishment and motivation as you see debts being eliminated.

3. Debt Consolidation: Debt consolidation involves combining multiple debts into a single loan with a lower interest rate. This can make it easier to manage and repay your debt. Options for debt consolidation include balance transfer credit cards, personal loans, or home equity loans. However, it's important to carefully evaluate the terms, fees, and interest rates associated with consolidation options to ensure it will truly benefit your financial situation.

4. Negotiate Lower Interest Rates: Contact your creditors and try to negotiate lower interest rates on your existing debts. Explain your financial situation and provide evidence of your ability to make regular payments. Some creditors may be willing to reduce interest rates to help you repay the debt. This can significantly lower your overall interest costs and accelerate your debt repayment.

5. Debt Management Plan: If you find it challenging to manage multiple debts on your own, consider working with a non-profit credit counseling agency. They can help you create a debt management plan (DMP) that consolidates your debts and negotiates reduced interest rates with your creditors. Under a

DMP, you make a single monthly payment to the credit counseling agency, which then distributes the funds to your creditors. This can simplify your debt repayment and help you become debt-free faster.

6. Increase Income and Reduce Expenses: Consider ways to increase your income, such as taking on a part-time job, freelancing, or selling unused items. Use the additional income to make extra debt payments. Additionally, look for opportunities to reduce your expenses by cutting back on discretionary spending, finding more affordable alternatives, or renegotiating contracts or subscriptions.

7. Seek Professional Advice: If you're overwhelmed by your debt or struggling to make progress, it may be beneficial to consult with a financial advisor or debt counselor. They can provide personalized advice and guidance based on your specific financial situation.

Remember, managing and reducing debt takes time and discipline. It's important to stay committed to your debt repayment plan and avoid incurring new debt. Celebrate small victories along the way and stay focused on your long-term financial goals. By implementing these techniques and adopting healthy financial habits, you can regain control of your finances and work towards a debt-free future.

**C. Insights on developing a debt repayment plan and staying motivated throughout the process**

Developing a debt repayment plan and staying motivated throughout the process can be challenging, but with the right strategies, you can achieve your financial goals. Here are some insights to help you:

1. Assess Your Debt: Start by gathering all the necessary information about your debts, including the outstanding balances, interest rates, and minimum payments. This will give you a clear understanding of your total debt and help you

prioritize which debts to tackle first.

2. Set Specific Goals: Establish clear and specific debt repayment goals. For example, you may aim to pay off a certain amount of debt within a specific time frame or target a specific debt to eliminate. Having specific goals will help you stay focused and motivated throughout the process.

3. Create a Realistic Budget: Develop a budget that aligns with your debt repayment goals. Identify areas where you can cut back on expenses and allocate more money towards debt repayment. Be realistic about your expenses and make sure your budget is sustainable in the long term. This will ensure that you have enough funds to cover your living expenses while making progress on your debt.

4. Choose a Debt Repayment Strategy: There are different strategies you can choose from to repay your debt. The debt snowball method involves paying off the smallest debt first while making minimum payments on other debts. The debt avalanche method focuses on paying off debts with the highest interest rates first. Evaluate these strategies and choose the one that aligns with your financial situation and motivates you the most.

5. Track Your Progress: Keep track of your debt repayment progress. This can be done through a spreadsheet, a debt tracking app, or even a visual representation like a debt repayment chart. Seeing your progress visually can be motivating and provide a sense of accomplishment as you check off debts that have been paid off.

6. Celebrate Milestones: Celebrate each milestone you reach in your debt repayment journey. Whether it's paying off a certain percentage of your debt or reaching a specific milestone, reward yourself for your hard work and progress. This can help you stay motivated and continue on your debt repayment path.

7. Find Support: Seek support from friends, family, or online

communities who are also on a debt repayment journey. Share your progress, challenges, and successes with them. They can provide encouragement, accountability, and helpful tips along the way. Sometimes, having someone to share your journey with can make a big difference.

8. Focus on the Long-Term Benefits: Remind yourself of the long-term benefits of becoming debt-free. Think about the financial freedom, reduced stress, and increased opportunities that await you once you're debt-free. Keep your eyes on the prize and use it as motivation during challenging times.

9. Practice Self-Care: Taking care of yourself physically and emotionally is important during the debt repayment process. Make sure to prioritize self-care activities like exercise, meditation, spending time with loved ones, and pursuing hobbies. These activities will help you stay balanced and motivated throughout your journey.

Remember, developing a debt repayment plan and staying motivated requires patience and perseverance. Stay committed to your goals, stay focused on your progress, and celebrate your achievements along the way. With determination and the right strategies, you can successfully repay your debt and achieve financial freedom.

# VIII. Chapter 7: Increasing Income

### A. Exploration of ways to increase income beyond the regular paycheck

Exploring ways to increase your income beyond your regular paycheck can provide additional financial stability and help you achieve your financial goals faster. Here are some ideas to consider:

1. Freelancing or Consulting: If you have a specific skill or expertise, consider offering your services as a freelancer or

consultant. This could be in areas such as writing, graphic design, web development, marketing, photography, or consulting in your industry. Freelancing allows you to work on projects outside of your regular job and earn extra income.

2. Starting a Side Business: If you have an entrepreneurial spirit, starting a side business can be a great way to generate additional income. Identify a market need or a hobby you are passionate about, and explore the possibility of turning it into a business. This could include selling products online, offering a service, or even starting a small local business.

3. Renting Out Assets: Do you have assets that are not being fully utilized? Consider renting them out to earn extra income. This could include renting out a spare room on platforms like Airbnb, renting out a parking space, or even renting out equipment or tools that you don't use frequently.

4. Monetizing Your Hobbies or Skills: If you have a hobby or skill that you enjoy, explore ways to monetize it. For example, if you enjoy crafting, you could sell your handmade items online or at local markets. If you are skilled in a particular sport or activity, you could offer lessons or coaching services.

5. Investing: Investing your money wisely can generate passive income over time. Explore different investment options such as stocks, bonds, real estate, or peer-to-peer lending platforms. It's important to do thorough research and seek professional advice before making any investment decisions.

6. Renting Out Your Property: If you own a property, consider renting out a portion of it. This could include renting out a room, a basement apartment, or even your entire property when you are away. Renting out your property can provide a steady stream of income.

7. Online Surveys and Microtasks: There are several platforms that offer paid online surveys and microtasks. While the income from

these activities may be relatively small, they can add up over time and require minimal effort. Just be cautious of scams and only sign up for reputable platforms.

8. Teaching or Tutoring: If you have expertise in a particular subject, consider offering tutoring services or teaching classes. This could be done in person or online. You could offer academic tutoring, language lessons, music lessons, or any other skill you excel in.

9. Passive Income Streams: Look for opportunities to create passive income streams. This could include writing an e-book, creating and selling digital products, investing in dividend-paying stocks, or creating a popular YouTube channel.

10. Taking on Gig Economy Jobs: Explore gig economy platforms that offer flexible work opportunities. This could include driving for ride-sharing services, delivering groceries, or completing tasks on platforms like TaskRabbit.

Remember, increasing your income beyond your regular paycheck requires dedication, time management, and sometimes taking risks. Consider your skills, interests, and available resources to find the best income-boosting opportunities for you.

**B. Suggestions for side hustles, freelancing, or entrepreneurship**

Here are some specific suggestions for side hustles, freelancing, or entrepreneurship:

1. Virtual Assistant: Offer your administrative and organizational skills as a virtual assistant. Many businesses and entrepreneurs are in need of help with tasks such as email management, scheduling, social media management, and research.

2. Content Writing or Copywriting: If you have strong writing skills, consider offering your services as a content writer or copywriter. Businesses often need help with creating blog posts,

website content, marketing materials, and product descriptions.

3. Graphic Design: If you have a talent for graphic design, offer your services to businesses or individuals in need of logos, branding materials, social media graphics, or website design.

4. Web Development: If you have coding skills, consider offering web development services. Many businesses and individuals require assistance with building or updating their websites.

5. Photography: If you have a passion for photography, offer your services for events, portraits, or product photography. You can also sell your photos online through stock photography platforms.

6. Social Media Management: Many businesses struggle to manage their social media presence effectively. Offer your expertise in managing and growing social media accounts for businesses.

7. Online Coaching or Consulting: If you have expertise in a specific area, such as fitness, nutrition, career development, or personal finance, consider offering online coaching or consulting services. This can be done through one-on-one sessions or group programs.

8. E-commerce: Start an online store and sell products that align with your interests or expertise. You can source products from wholesalers, create your own products, or use print-on-demand services.

9. Event Planning: If you have strong organizational and planning skills, offer your services as an event planner for weddings, parties, or corporate events.

10. Language Tutoring: If you are fluent in a second language, offer language tutoring services either in person or online. Many individuals are eager to learn new languages for personal or professional reasons.

Remember to identify your strengths, passions, and skills when choosing a side hustle, freelancing gig, or entrepreneurial venture. It's important to focus on something you enjoy and are good at to increase your chances of success.

### C. Guidance on developing new skills or seeking career advancement opportunities

Here are some suggestions for developing new skills and seeking career advancement opportunities:

1. Identify your Goals: Start by identifying your career goals and the skills you need to achieve them. This will help you focus your efforts and choose the right areas to develop.

2. Assess Your Current Skills: Take stock of your existing skills and knowledge. Identify any gaps that need to be filled in order to reach your goals.

3. Continuous Learning: Commit to lifelong learning to stay relevant and competitive in your field. Take advantage of online courses, workshops, webinars, and industry conferences to acquire new skills and knowledge.

4. Seek Mentorship: Find someone in your industry who can serve as a mentor. They can provide guidance, share their experiences, and help you navigate your career path.

5. Networking: Build a strong professional network by attending industry events, joining professional organizations, and connecting with colleagues and industry experts on platforms like LinkedIn. Networking can open doors to new opportunities and provide valuable insights.

6. Take on New Projects: Seek out opportunities to take on new projects or assignments that allow you to develop new skills. Volunteer for cross-functional teams, offer to lead a project, or take on additional responsibilities that align with your career

goals.

7. Seek Feedback: Be open to receiving feedback from colleagues, supervisors, and mentors. Constructive feedback can help you identify areas for improvement and guide your skill development.

8. Professional Certifications: Research professional certifications that are relevant to your field. These certifications can enhance your credibility and demonstrate your expertise to employers.

9. Update Your Resume and Online Presence: Keep your resume and online profiles up to date with your latest skills, accomplishments, and experiences. This will help you stand out to potential employers and showcase your growth.

10. Explore New Roles or Industries: Consider exploring new roles or industries that align with your interests and offer growth opportunities. This may involve a career change or transitioning to a different department within your current organization.

Remember, developing new skills and seeking career advancement is a continuous process. It requires dedication, persistence, and a willingness to adapt to change. Stay proactive, seize opportunities, and always be open to learning and growth.

# IX. Chapter 8: Changing Mindset and Habits

## A. Importance of mindset shifts in achieving financial stability

Mindset shifts play a crucial role in achieving financial stability. Here are some reasons why mindset shifts are important:

1. Overcoming Limiting Beliefs: Mindset shifts help you overcome limiting beliefs about money and wealth. It's essential to challenge negative beliefs such as "money is scarce" or "I'm not good with finances" and replace them with positive and empowering beliefs that support financial stability.

2. Building a Growth Mindset: Adopting a growth mindset is vital for financial stability. This mindset emphasizes the belief that you can learn, improve, and develop the skills necessary to manage your finances effectively. It enables you to embrace challenges, persist in the face of setbacks, and continuously seek opportunities for growth.

3. Developing Financial Discipline: A mindset shift can help you develop the discipline needed to make wise financial decisions. It involves prioritizing long-term financial goals over short-term gratification, practicing delayed gratification, and making conscious choices that align with your financial objectives.

4. Embracing Financial Education: A mindset shift involves recognizing the importance of financial education and actively seeking knowledge about personal finance. It encourages you to invest time and effort in learning about budgeting, saving, investing, and other financial concepts. With a growth mindset, you are open to acquiring new skills and knowledge to improve your financial situation.

5. Taking Ownership of Finances: Mindset shifts empower you to take full ownership of your financial situation. Instead of blaming external factors or circumstances, you recognize that you have control over your financial choices and actions. This mindset enables you to become proactive in managing your money, setting financial goals, and making intentional decisions that lead to stability and success.

6. Embracing a Long-Term Perspective: A mindset shift involves shifting from a short-term focus to a long-term perspective when it comes to finances. It means understanding the importance of saving for emergencies, retirement, and future financial goals. By prioritizing long-term financial stability, you can make decisions that align with your future financial well-being.

7. Cultivating Financial Resilience: Mindset shifts help you

develop resilience in the face of financial challenges. Instead of being overwhelmed by setbacks or setbacks, you approach them as opportunities for growth and learning. This resilience enables you to bounce back from financial setbacks, adapt to changes, and find creative solutions to financial problems.

In summary, mindset shifts are essential for achieving financial stability as they enable you to overcome limiting beliefs, develop financial discipline, embrace education, take ownership of your finances, adopt a long-term perspective, and cultivate resilience. By shifting your mindset, you can create a solid foundation for financial stability and success.

**B. Strategies for overcoming limiting beliefs and adopting positive money habits**

Overcoming limiting beliefs and adopting positive money habits is crucial for achieving financial stability. Here are some strategies to help you:

1. Identify and Challenge Limiting Beliefs: Start by identifying any limiting beliefs you have about money. These beliefs may include thoughts such as "I'll never be wealthy" or "Money is the root of all evil." Once you've identified these beliefs, challenge them by questioning their validity and replacing them with positive and empowering beliefs. For example, replace "I'll never be wealthy" with "I have the ability to create wealth through smart financial decisions."

2. Surround Yourself with Positive Influences: Surround yourself with people who have a positive mindset towards money and financial success. Engage in conversations with individuals who are financially successful and learn from their experiences. This can help you shift your perspective and adopt a more positive mindset towards money.

3. Educate Yourself: Take the time to educate yourself about personal finance. Read books, attend seminars or workshops, and

follow reputable financial experts. By gaining knowledge about money management, investing, and budgeting, you can build confidence and make informed decisions about your finances.

4. Set Clear Financial Goals: Define your financial goals and create a plan to achieve them. Setting clear and measurable goals helps you stay focused and motivated. Break down your goals into smaller, actionable steps and track your progress regularly. Celebrate your achievements along the way, which reinforces positive money habits.

5. Practice Gratitude and Abundance: Cultivate a mindset of gratitude and abundance. Instead of focusing on what you lack, appreciate what you already have. Practice gratitude for the money you earn, the resources available to you, and the opportunities that come your way. This shift in mindset helps attract more abundance into your life.

6. Create a Budget and Track Expenses: Establish a budget that aligns with your financial goals and values. Track your expenses and analyze where your money is going. This helps you identify areas where you can cut back and save more. By having a clear understanding of your finances, you can make conscious decisions and develop positive money habits.

7. Practice Delayed Gratification: Learn to delay instant gratification and prioritize long-term financial goals. Avoid impulsive purchases and instead, focus on saving and investing for the future. This requires discipline and self-control, but it can lead to significant financial stability and success.

8. Celebrate Small Wins: Acknowledge and celebrate small financial achievements along the way. Whether it's paying off a debt, reaching a savings milestone, or sticking to your budget, recognizing your progress reinforces positive money habits and motivates you to continue on your financial journey.

Remember, overcoming limiting beliefs and adopting positive

money habits is a journey that takes time and effort. Be patient with yourself and focus on making incremental changes. With persistence and a positive mindset, you can transform your financial life and achieve long-term stability.

## C. Techniques for cultivating discipline, patience, and financial resilience

Cultivating discipline, patience, and financial resilience is key to achieving financial success. Here are some techniques to help you develop these qualities:

1. Set Clear and Specific Goals: Define your financial goals and make them clear and specific. Whether it's saving for a down payment on a house, paying off debt, or building an emergency fund, having a clear target helps you stay focused and motivated. Write down your goals and regularly review them to remind yourself of what you're working towards.

2. Create a Budget and Stick to It: Establishing a budget is essential for managing your finances effectively. It helps you allocate your income towards different expenses and savings goals. Create a realistic budget that aligns with your financial goals and stick to it. Track your expenses, avoid unnecessary spending, and make adjustments as needed. Discipline yourself to follow the budget consistently.

3. Practice Delayed Gratification: Develop the ability to delay instant gratification and prioritize long-term financial goals. Instead of giving in to impulsive purchases, take the time to evaluate whether a purchase aligns with your financial priorities. Consider whether it will bring long-term value or if the money could be better utilized elsewhere. By practicing delayed gratification, you can make more thoughtful financial decisions and avoid unnecessary debt.

4. Build an Emergency Fund: Financial resilience involves being prepared for unexpected expenses or emergencies. Start building

an emergency fund by setting aside a portion of your income regularly. Aim to accumulate three to six months' worth of living expenses. Having an emergency fund provides a safety net and reduces the need to rely on credit cards or loans during challenging times.

5. Automate Savings and Investments: Make saving and investing a priority by automating the process. Set up automatic transfers from your checking account to a savings or investment account. This ensures that a portion of your income is consistently allocated towards your financial goals, even if you're tempted to spend it. Automating savings and investments helps build discipline and makes it easier to stick to your financial plan.

6. Practice Mindful Spending: Cultivate mindfulness when it comes to your spending habits. Before making a purchase, ask yourself if it aligns with your values and financial goals. Consider whether it is a need or a want. By being mindful of your spending, you can avoid unnecessary expenses and make more intentional choices with your money.

7. Educate Yourself about Personal Finance: Take the time to educate yourself about personal finance concepts, such as budgeting, investing, and debt management. Read books, articles, and listen to podcasts from reputable sources. The more knowledge you have, the better equipped you'll be to make informed financial decisions. Continuous learning helps build patience and resilience as you navigate the ups and downs of your financial journey.

8. Practice Self-Care and Stress Management: Taking care of your physical and mental well-being is crucial for maintaining discipline, patience, and financial resilience. Engage in activities that help you relax and reduce stress, such as exercise, meditation, or spending time with loved ones. Prioritize self-care to stay motivated and resilient during financial challenges.

Remember, developing discipline, patience, and financial

resilience is a continuous process. It requires commitment and consistency. Be patient with yourself, celebrate small wins along the way, and keep your long-term financial goals in mind. With time and practice, these qualities will become ingrained in your financial habits, leading to greater financial stability and success.

# X. Chapter 9: Building a Sustainable Financial Future

### A. Advice on long-term financial planning, including retirement savings and investments

Long-term financial planning, especially for retirement savings and investments, is crucial for securing a comfortable future. Here are some key pieces of advice to consider:

1. Start Early: The earlier you start saving for retirement, the better. Time is your greatest asset when it comes to long-term investments. The power of compounding allows your money to grow exponentially over time. Even small contributions can make a significant difference if given enough time to grow.

2. Assess Your Financial Goals: Determine your retirement goals and estimate the amount of money you'll need to achieve them. Consider factors such as your desired lifestyle, healthcare costs, and inflation. This will help you set a target for your retirement savings and guide your investment strategy.

3. Contribute to Retirement Accounts: Take advantage of retirement accounts such as employer-sponsored 401(k) plans or individual retirement accounts (IRAs). These accounts offer tax advantages that can boost your savings. Contribute the maximum amount allowed, especially if your employer offers a matching contribution.

4. Diversify Your Investments: Spread your investments across different asset classes to reduce risk. Diversification helps protect

your portfolio from major fluctuations in any one investment. Consider a mix of stocks, bonds, mutual funds, and other investment vehicles that align with your risk tolerance and long-term goals.

5. Regularly Review and Adjust Your Investments: Monitor your investments regularly to ensure they are aligned with your goals and risk tolerance. Rebalance your portfolio periodically to maintain the desired asset allocation. As you approach retirement, consider gradually shifting your investments to a more conservative approach to safeguard your savings.

6. Seek Professional Advice: Consider consulting with a financial advisor or planner who specializes in retirement planning. They can help you create a personalized plan based on your specific circumstances and goals. A professional can provide valuable insights, guidance, and help you navigate complex financial decisions.

7. Continuously Educate Yourself: Stay informed about financial trends, market conditions, and retirement planning strategies. Attend seminars, read books, and follow reputable financial sources. The more knowledge you have, the better equipped you'll be to make informed decisions about your retirement savings and investments.

8. Plan for Healthcare Costs: Take into account the potential costs of healthcare during retirement. As you age, healthcare expenses may increase. Consider purchasing long-term care insurance or exploring other options to protect yourself financially from unexpected medical costs.

9. Prepare for Social Security and Pension Benefits: Understand how Social Security and any pension benefits you may be entitled to will factor into your retirement income. Familiarize yourself with the eligibility requirements and projected benefits. Consider the optimal time to start receiving Social Security payments based on your individual circumstances.

10. Regularly Review Your Plan: Life circumstances and financial goals can change over time. Regularly review and update your long-term financial plan to ensure it remains relevant and aligned with your objectives. Make adjustments as needed to stay on track towards your retirement goals.

Remember, long-term financial planning requires patience, discipline, and regular monitoring. Be proactive, stay committed to saving and investing for the long term, and seek professional advice when needed. By taking these steps, you can increase the likelihood of achieving a secure and comfortable retirement.

**B. Tips for maintaining financial discipline and avoiding the paycheck-to-paycheck cycle in the future**

1. Create a Budget: Start by tracking your income and expenses to gain a clear understanding of your financial situation. Create a budget that allocates your income towards essential expenses, savings, and debt repayment. Stick to your budget and avoid overspending.

2. Build an Emergency Fund: Establishing an emergency fund is crucial to handle unexpected expenses without resorting to debt. Aim to save three to six months' worth of living expenses in a separate savings account. Start small and set aside a portion of your income regularly until you reach your goal.

3. Cut Unnecessary Expenses: Review your expenses and identify areas where you can cut back. Eliminate or reduce discretionary expenses like dining out, entertainment, or subscription services that you can live without. Redirect the money saved towards savings or debt repayment.

4. Prioritize Debt Repayment: If you have high-interest debts, such as credit card debt, prioritize paying them off. Consider using the debt snowball or debt avalanche method to systematically tackle your debts. Make consistent payments and avoid taking on new

debt whenever possible.

5. Live Below Your Means: Avoid the temptation to increase your spending every time your income increases. Instead, maintain a lifestyle that is below your means. This will allow you to save more, pay off debt faster, and build wealth over time.

6. Automate Savings and Bill Payments: Set up automatic transfers to your savings account and automate bill payments. This ensures that you consistently save and pay your bills on time, reducing the risk of late fees or missed payments.

7. Avoid Impulse Purchases: Before making a purchase, take a moment to evaluate whether it is a necessity or a want. Avoid impulsive buying decisions and give yourself time to think before making non-essential purchases. Consider implementing a waiting period (e.g., 24 hours) for significant purchases to avoid buyer's remorse.

8. Seek Financial Education: Invest time in improving your financial literacy. Read books, attend seminars, or take online courses to enhance your knowledge about personal finance. The more you understand about managing money, the better equipped you'll be to make sound financial decisions.

9. Set Realistic Goals: Establish short-term and long-term financial goals to stay motivated. Whether it's saving for a down payment on a house, paying off student loans, or building a retirement nest egg, having clear goals can help you stay focused and committed to financial discipline.

10. Surround Yourself with Supportive Influences: Surround yourself with people who share your financial values and goals. Seek support from friends, family, or online communities focused on personal finance. Sharing experiences and learning from others can help you stay motivated and accountable.

Remember, achieving financial discipline takes time and effort. Be patient with yourself and celebrate small victories along the way. By implementing these tips consistently, you can break the cycle of living paycheck to paycheck and build a solid foundation for a more secure financial future.

### C. Stories of individuals who successfully broke free from living paycheck to paycheck

Here are a few inspiring stories of individuals who successfully broke free from living paycheck to paycheck:

1. The Frugal Family: Sarah and Mark were a couple struggling to make ends meet while raising their two children. They decided to make a change and adopted a frugal lifestyle. They cut unnecessary expenses, cooked meals at home, and negotiated better deals on utilities. They also started a side business selling handmade crafts online. Over time, their savings grew, and they were able to pay off debt and build an emergency fund. Today, they live comfortably and enjoy financial security.

2. The Debt Crusher: John was burdened with significant credit card debt and living paycheck to paycheck. He decided to take control of his finances and created a budget to track his income and expenses. John took on a part-time job to increase his income and used the extra money to pay off his debts aggressively. He also negotiated lower interest rates with his creditors. Through discipline and determination, John paid off all his debts within a few years and transformed his financial situation.

3. The Side Hustler: Lisa had a stable job but struggled to save money. She started exploring side hustle opportunities to increase her income. Lisa began freelancing as a graphic designer in her spare time. She used the additional income to build an emergency fund and pay off her student loans. Eventually, her side hustle grew into a full-time business, allowing her to quit her job and achieve financial freedom.

4. The Budgeting Guru: David was tired of living paycheck to

paycheck and not having any savings. He decided to take a deep dive into his finances and learned about budgeting and money management. David created a detailed budget, cut unnecessary expenses, and started tracking every penny. He also learned about investing and started putting aside money for retirement. With his newfound financial discipline, David was able to break free from the paycheck-to-paycheck cycle and build a solid financial foundation.

5. The Minimalist Journey: Sarah and Mike were overwhelmed by their cluttered lifestyle and financial stress. They embraced minimalism and downsized their possessions and living space. By adopting a minimalist mindset, they reduced their expenses and focused on experiences rather than material possessions. This allowed them to save more, pay off debts, and eventually achieve financial freedom.

These stories highlight the power of determination, discipline, and strategic financial planning. By making small changes, setting goals, and staying focused, these individuals were able to break free from the paycheck-to-paycheck cycle and create a more secure financial future.

# XI. Conclusion

### A. Encouragement and motivation for readers to take action towards financial freedom

Achieving financial freedom is a worthy goal, and taking action towards it can be empowering. Here are some words of encouragement and motivation to inspire you on your journey:

1. Believe in yourself: Have confidence in your abilities and believe that you have the potential to achieve financial freedom. Your mindset and self-belief are crucial for taking action and overcoming challenges.

2. Set clear goals: Define your financial goals and create a

roadmap to reach them. Break them down into smaller, achievable milestones that you can work towards. Having a clear vision will keep you motivated and focused.

3. Educate yourself: Take the time to learn about personal finance, investing, and money management. Knowledge is power, and the more you understand about financial matters, the better equipped you'll be to make informed decisions and take effective action.

4. Take control of your spending: Evaluate your expenses and identify areas where you can cut back or eliminate unnecessary costs. Create a budget and stick to it, prioritizing your financial goals over impulsive spending.

5. Save and invest wisely: Develop a habit of saving a portion of your income regularly. Explore different investment options that align with your risk tolerance and financial goals. Start early and be consistent in your savings and investment efforts.

6. Embrace a growth mindset: View setbacks or failures as learning opportunities rather than reasons to give up. Stay adaptable and open to new strategies and ideas. Remember that financial freedom is a journey, and it may require adjustments along the way.

7. Surround yourself with like-minded individuals: Connect with people who share similar goals and aspirations. Join financial communities, attend seminars or workshops, or seek out mentors who can inspire and guide you on your path to financial freedom.

8. Celebrate your progress: Acknowledge and celebrate your achievements, no matter how small they may seem. Recognize the steps you've taken towards financial freedom and use them as motivation to keep pushing forward.

Remember, taking action towards financial freedom requires consistency, discipline, and patience. Stay committed to your goals, and with time and effort, you can achieve the financial freedom you desire.

Dear Readers,

I hope this message finds you well. I wanted to take a moment to express my sincere gratitude for your continued support and readership. Your engagement and enthusiasm have been truly inspiring, and it is because of you that I am able to pursue my passion for writing and sharing valuable information.

I strive to provide content that is informative, relevant, and helpful to you. Your satisfaction is my top priority, which is why I am reaching out today to kindly request your honest review. Your feedback is incredibly valuable in helping me understand what I'm doing well and what areas I can improve upon.

I greatly appreciate any comments, suggestions, or constructive criticism you may have. Your insights will not only assist me in enhancing the quality of my content but also ensure that I am addressing topics that truly resonate with you, my readers.

Once again, thank you for being a part of this journey. Your continued support and feedback are invaluable to me. I am committed to delivering content that adds value to your life, and your honest review will help me achieve that goal.

With heartfelt appreciation,

M. Livingston

www.ingramcontent.com/pod-product-compliance
Lightning Source LLC
Chambersburg PA
CBHW062300290526
45794CB00006B/2632